The

Imperfect

Paradise

by *LINDA PASTAN*

A Perfect Circle of Sun
Aspects of Eve
The Five Stages of Grief
Waiting for My Life
PM/AM: New and Selected Poems
A Fraction of Darkness

The Imperfect Paradise

Poems by
LINDA PASTAN

W · W · NORTON & COMPANY · NEW YORK · LONDON

I would like to thank the following periodicals in which these poems first appeared:

The Agni Review; The American Voice; The Atlantic Monthly; Crosscurrents; The Denver Quarterly; The Georgia Review; Gettysburg Review; Grand Street; The New Republic; Nimrod; The Paris Review; The Pennsylvania Review; Ploughshares; Poetry; The Radcliffe Quarterly; The Sonora Review; Southern Poetry Review; Tri Quarterly; The Virginia Quarterly Review.

The text of this book is composed in Gael, with display type set in Bulmer. Composition and manufacturing by The Haddon Craftsmen, Inc.

First Edition

Library of Congress Cataloging-in-Publication Data

Pastan, Linda, 1932–
   The imperfect paradise. Poems.

   I. Title.
PS3566.A775I47 1988 811'.54 87-24889

ISBN 0-393-02565-9

W. W. Norton & Company, Inc., 500 Fifth Avenue, New York, N. Y. 10110
W. W. Norton & Company Ltd., 37 Great Russell Street, London WC1B 3NU

1 2 3 4 5 6 7 8 9 0

In Memory of My Mother
Bess Olenik

and for
Nicholas Olenik Pastan

Contents

4. The Descent   49

5. The Imperfect Paradise   69

We have all been expelled from the Garden, but the ones who suffer most in exile are those who are still permitted to dream of perfection.

Stanley Kunitz
"Seedcorn and Windfall"
from *Next to Last Things*

The imperfect is our paradise

Wallace Stevens
"The Poems of Our Climate"

1. In the Rearview Mirror

Bird on Bough

". . . the bird on a branch
painted by some Sung
academician is a symbol to
express what we might call
the bird-on-bough aspect of
eternity."

                    The Arts of China,
                        Michael Sullivan

On a branch
somewhere in eternity
a bird sits,

each
feather
one silhouette

of the brush
laid flat
on the page,

each leaf
a single
grace note.

Is it a cardinal on willow,
or a dove on peach?
No matter.

Years ago
far from China
I saw

the same bird
on the same bough—
a sparrow perhaps,

sooty
as coal dust traced
with a finger.

There,
in the eternity
that is childhood

was the branch
which would neither grow
nor break

and the solitary bird
which would never
fly away.

Grudnow

When he spoke of where he came from,
my grandfather could have been
clearing his throat
of that name, that town
sometimes Poland, sometimes Russia,
the borders pencilled in
with a hand as shaky as his.
He left, I heard him say,
because there was nothing there.

I understood what he meant
when I saw the photograph
of his people standing
against a landscape emptied
of crops and trees, scraped raw
by winter. Everything
was in sepia, as if the brown earth
had stained the faces,
stained even the air.

I would have died there, I think
in childhood maybe
of some fever,
my face pressed for warmth
against a cow with flanks
like those of the great aunts
in the picture. Or later
I would have died of history
like the others, who dug

their stubborn heels into that earth,
heels as hard as the heels
of the bread my grandfather tore
from the loaf at supper. He always
sipped his tea through a cube of sugar
clenched in his teeth, the way
he sipped his life here, noisily,
through all he remembered
that might have been sweet in Grudnow.

To a Daughter Leaving Home

When I taught you
at eight to ride
a bicycle, loping along
beside you
as you wobbled away
on two round wheels,
my own mouth rounding
in surprise when you pulled
ahead down the curved
path of the park,
I kept waiting
for the thud
of your crash as I
sprinted to catch up,
while you grew
smaller, more breakable
with distance,
pumping, pumping
for your life, screaming
with laughter,
the hair flapping
behind you like a
handkerchief waving
goodbye.

The Dogwoods

I remember, in the week
of the dogwoods, why sometimes
we give up everything
for beauty, lose our sense
and our senses, as we do now
for these blossoms, sprinkled
like salt through the dark woods.

And like the story of pheasants
with salt on their tails
to tame them,
look how we are made helpless
by a brief explosion
of petals
one week in April.

Root Pruning

Years before you moved
that holly from the woods
into the place that waited
at the garden's edge,
you dug your shovel in
around its roots
every time we took a walk
that way. Root pruning,
you said. The garden waited.
Seasons came and went
and layers of leaves
like old linoleum
accumulated every year.
I'd even forget
just what it was we waited for,
although you used your shovel
like a walking stick,
carrying it with you
almost every day.

Years have gone by,
the holly shades
our daughter's window now.
Sometimes I believe
if I had done any one thing
in some other way
everything would be fine,
and we would be happy
the way families are
whose innocence goes with them
to the grave, who mourn
each other, when they must,

with no regrets.
If you had root pruned me,
if I had known some cutting edge
during all those years,
maybe I wouldn't feel now
as if the ground had simply
disappeared.

After an Absence

After an absence that was no one's fault
we are shy with each other,
and our words seem younger than we are,
as if we must return to the time we met
and work ourselves back to the present,
the way you never read a story
from the place you stopped
but always start each book all over again.
Perhaps we should have stayed
tied like mountain climbers
by the safe cord of the phone,
its dial our own small prayer wheel,
our voices less ghostly across the miles,
less awkward than they are now.
I had forgotten the grey in your curls,
that splash of winter over your face,
remembering the younger man
you used to be.

And I feel myself turn old and ordinary,
having to think again of food for supper,
the animals to be tended, the whole riptide
of daily life hidden but perilous
pulling both of us under so fast.
I have dreamed of our bed
as if it were a shore where we would be washed up,
not this striped mattress
we must cover with sheets. I had forgotten
all the old business between us,
like mail unanswered so long that silence
becomes eloquent, a message of its own.
I had even forgotten how married love
is a territory more mysterious

the more it is explored, like one of those terrains
you read about, a garden in the desert
where you stoop to drink, never knowing
if your mouth will fill with water or sand.

Beauty Shop

What is sweeter than honey?
What is stronger than a lion?
                    Samson to the Philistines

1.

Named for the archangel Michael
this twice born barber
snips my hair, his scissors
describing a halo
around my head
as if I were to be a nun
or Jewish bride.

2.

I had forgotten
the shape
of the skull
defined
by a wet comb
and how my grandmother
braided my hair
so hard my eyes would ache.
She wore, in a silver locket
at her throat, the hair
of her long-dead child.

3.

In this place perfumed
with flowers
and singed hair, girls
with the lowered eyes
of penitents
make of each woman's nails
a row of shields.

4.

We are dreaming
of transformations,
of walking
into the world
somebody else.

5.

In Rome once
standing before Titian's
Sacred And Profane Love,
I gazed at the women
each coiffed
in that luminous paint
and wondered
which was which.

6.

I used to cut
my lover's hair myself.
Curls as delicate
as shaved wood
covered the floor,
and later the swaying curtain
of my hair
was all there was
between us.

7.

Hair line crack . . .
Hair trigger . . . Hair shirt . . .
I cross a palm
with silver
and sense the pillars
shake.

Ceremony

You are as faithful a widow
as you were a wife,
celebrating black

marking each anniversary
of death, marriage, and birth
until the calendar

blooms with occasions
like a perpetual funeral
wreath.

Perhaps you can domesticate
anything,
teaching pain

to heel at command,
lick your face with its rough tongue,
eat from your plate.

Even the empty
place
at the table

can be a simple
ceremony
of absence.

So that afterwards
when the night closes
its dark petals around you

the music
of your voice
speaking to itself

becomes
a duet
with silence.

Snapshot of My Mother at 15

Sometimes in photographs
or deep in mirrors
I sense a disturbance
in the molecules—a flick
of the past or the future.
In this picture for instance
the face of the woman stirs
behind the face of the girl,
the way beneath the surface of a lake
the shadow of a fish slides by.

My mother's skin
as smooth as water here
will wrinkle as water does
over stones, the widow's peak
fulfill its prophecy. My surgeon father
could peel back membranes
layer by fragile layer,
like my mother turning down
a bed. There are depths
whose measure we only guess.

Turnabout

The old dog used to herd me through the street
As if the leash were for my benefit,
And when our walk was over he would sit
A friendly jailer, zealous, at my feet.
My children would pretend that they felt fine
When I was anxious at some hurt of theirs
As if they were the parents, for the tears
At their predicaments were often mine.

And now against the whiteness of the sheet
My mother, white faced, comforts with the story
of Brahms, the boy, who couldn't sleep for worry
Until a chord achieved its harmony,
So down the stairs he crept to play the C.
She means her death will make a circle complete.

At Xian

A farmer digging a well in central China
uncovered the site where 6ooo terra cotta
soldiers were buried by the first Chin emperor. . . .
                                        guided tour

How we would love to take
the things of this world with us
to the next: a wife,
a well-thumbed book, something
in gold, perhaps, to mimic sunlight.
This emperor took a whole clay army,
each soldier as large
as life or larger, each separate face
the remnant of a man
who has become wholly artifact.
Was it a matter of wanting
to fall asleep safe—the dark
held back by bronze torches,
by kneeling archers with bows
the shape of half moons
who watched all night, who took
the weight of the dense earth
on their perfect shoulders?
Maybe it's only the numbers
we can't comprehend . . . thousand
upon thousand . . . the way
we misconstrue the whole scale
of China. Or is it simply
the slaves and artisans we balk at,
planted live, mouths filled with dirt
to bury the secrets
of this buried place?
And what excavations
do we secretly long for,
our hearts emptied of plunder,

our wrist-bones bracelets
in some museum to come?
We bury our dead in silks
for the occasion, then leave them
to fend for themselves
in their small portions of earth,
though we too might send armies
if we could.

In the Rearview Mirror

Driving all night in winter,
I watch in the rearview mirror
as the small towns disappear
behind us, ceasing
to exist the moment
we pass. Hills rise and fall
brindled with snow,
and in the fields a few
lit windows small
as night lights
remind us of a child asleep
upstairs, the blanket rising
and falling with his breath.
How the particular
loses itself. Downstairs
the dough is rising
under its cloth, and the Mother
whose hands have learned
the wisdom of kneading
touches the Father.
And one town dims
and flickers out, and another
stirs ready to rise
three hundred miles later
when the sun touches the farthest edge
of the sky in an endless
relay race of light,
at a place half resurrected
from childhood and waiting
to be unwrapped like a withheld gift
from the white ribbon
of unwinding road.

2. Rereading
The Odyssey
in Middle Age

At the Loom

You sit at the loom,
your hands raised
like silhouetted birds,
or like a harpist poised
at the strings of an instrument
whose chords are colors,
their slow accumulation,
thread by thread—
a kind of bleeding upward
the way the sky bleeds
from the horizon up
after certain sunsets.
Monk's belt and rosepath . . .
plainweave and twill . . .
The shuttle moves back
and forth, trailing
its wake of yarn
as if by accident,
and patterns that seem
random at first multiply
into beauty.
No wonder Penelope burned
with patience.
Somewhere a sheep bleats
in the night, a silkworm
stirs in its cocoon.
You weave a spell,
I wear it on my back,
and though the chilly stars
go bone naked
we are clothed.

Rereading *The Odyssey* in Middle Age

Why was she weaving a shroud for Laertes,
and why have I thought for years
it was a shawl she made, something warm
a man might wrap around her shoulders
windy nights—one of the suitors, perhaps,
much younger than she and surely
younger than Odysseus.
Perhaps Laertes kept his eye on her
suspiciously. Did she mean
to finish it after all, unweaving
less and less each night, and could that mean
she wished Laertes dead? Yarns dyed the colors
of the sea: greens, purples, and hyacinth.
How can we hope to find the darker threads
of her impatience or lust
in the design of that nubby material?
We make our myths from whole cloth anyway
and make ourselves the heroines
of others' imaginings.

The shuttle was always moving back
and forth across the loom, as restless
as Odysseus himself, or any man.
I think of the uses of "shroud":
how the night can be shrouded in fog
in places like this one, near the sea;
how leaves in summer shroud each mother branch;
and how your husband's father looks at you
with wrinkled lids shrouding
those knowing eyes.
What is faithfulness anyway?
Penelope asks. Is the sea faithful
to the shore, whether it beats against it

or withdraws, leaving only a trace
of its commandment on the naked sand?
She wonders if Telemachus will find a wife
to weave a shroud for her lost
father-in-law, or would the water
be winding sheet enough for him?

Circe

I will always be the other woman.
I disappear
for a time
like the moon in daylight,
then rise at night all mother-of-pearl
so that a man's upturned face,
watching,
will have reflected on it
the milk of longing.

And though he may leave, memory
will perfect me.
One day the light
may fall in a certain way
on Penelope's hair,
and he will pause wildly . . .
but when she turns,
it will only be his wife, to whom
white sheets simply mean laundry—

even Nausikaä
in her silly braids
thought more of washing linen
than of him,
preferring Odysseus
clean and oiled
to that briny,
unkempt lion
I would choose.

Let Dido and her kind
leap from cliffs
for love.
My men will moan and dream of me
for years . . .
desire and need
become the same animal
in the silken
dark.

To be the other woman
is to be a season
that is always about to end,
when the air is flowered
with jasmine and peach,
and the weather day after day
is flawless,
and the forecast
is hurricane.

Argos

Shaggy and incontinent,
I have become the very legend
of fidelity. I am
more famous than the dog star
or those hounds of Charon's
who nip at a man's ankles
on his way to the underworld.
Even Penelope wanted
proof, and Eurykleia
had to see a scar.
But I knew what I knew—
what else are noses for?
Men are such needy creatures,
Zeus himself comes to them
as an animal. I'll take
my place gladly
among the bones and fleas
of this fragrant dung heap
and doze my doggy way
through history.

The Sirens

Is there no music now
except the chime
of coins in the pocket
for which a man would go breathlessly
off course, would even drown?
Odysseus tied to his mast
regretted his own foresight.

In ordinary days to come in Ithaca
the song of some distant bird,
the chords of water against
the shore, even Penelope
humming to herself at the loom
would make his head turn, his eyes
stray toward the sea.

The Son

"Then the thoughtful Telemachus said to her in answer:
. . . nobody really knows his own father."

The Odyssey, Book 1

If life is simply a lesson
in how we should have lived it,
perhaps the Odyssey was meant for Telemachus—
a kind of primer, a head start.
Even the parts about the mother distracted
at her loom, the dog whining on the doorsill,
and the kitchen so busy with ox and sheep
to feed the suitors, that the boy was told,
and told again, to play outside. When Athena
finally came to stir him up, he was like a child
whose toy bow has suddenly arched to the size
of a rainbow, as later the stranger's
would seem to, in the Great Hall.
After his own difficult journey—the men
all mocking him at first, real dangers
barely averted, his voice hoarsening
with manhood, even authority—
what it came down to in the end
was his wily father home at last,
perfection itself, and more
critical than in those boyish dreams
of rescue. The man even warned his son,
who had braved so much alone, not to shame
the blood of Odysseus. So was the lesson
Patience or Valor? Power or Wisdom?
Or was it simply family feeling:
long evenings to come in Ithaca, Penelope
weaving both men tunics, with only
hearth fires burning now. And stories,
Ah the stories! through the chilly nights.

The Suitor

There is always a story
that no one bothers to tell:
the younger son of a younger son,
hardly a suitor at all, sits
at the sharp edge of the table
among the boisterous men, not hungry
except for a glimpse of Penelope,
a woman wasted, he thinks—
those pale arms, that hair
a web she might have woven
around her own head.
Sometimes he tries to speak
to the son who looks at him wonderingly,
but doesn't answer.
How could Odysseus have left?
he asks himself, but is grateful
for the chance to pretend
it could be him she'll choose.
He almost knows it must end badly,
though his will be a minor tributary
in that unplumbed sea
of wasted blood.

3. Balancing Act

The Safecracker

On nights when the moon seems inpenetrable—
a locked porthole to space;
when the householder bars his windows
and doors, and his dog lies until dawn,
one jeweled eye open; when the maiden sleeps
with her rosy knees sealed tightly together,
on such nights the safecracker sets to work.
Axe . . . Chisel . . . Nitroglycerin . . .
Within the vault lie forty thousand
tons of gold; the heaped up spoils
of Ali Baba's cave; the secrets of the molecule.
He sands his fingertips
to feel the subtle vibrations
of wheel lining up, just so, with wheel.
His toolmarks are his fingerprints.
And now a crack appears on the side
of the egg, a single fault line,
and within: the golden yolk just waiting.
A kind of wind . . . a door flies open . . . a glitter
of forsythia forced out of the branch.
With smoothest fingertips you touch
the locked cage of my ribs . . . just so.
My knees fall open. And Cleopatra smiles,
whose own Egyptians first invented the lock.

Ars Poetica

1. *The Muse*

You may catch
a butterfly
in a net
if you are swift enough

or if you keep
perfectly still
perhaps it will land
on your shoulder.

Often
it is just
a moth.

2. *Writing*

In the battle
between the typewriter
and the blank page
a certain rhythm evolves,
not unlike the hoofbeats
of a horse groomed for war
who would rather be
head down, grazing.

3. *Rejection Slip*

Darling, though you know
I admire your many
fine qualities
you don't fill all my needs

just now, and besides
there's a backlog
waiting to fit
in my bed.

4. *Revision*

The tree has been green
all summer, but now
it tries red . . . copper . . .
even gold. Soon
leaf after leaf
will be discarded,
there will be nothing
but bare tree, soon
it will be almost time
to start over again.

5. *Ars poetica*

Escape from the poem
by bus, by streetcar—
any way you can,
dragging a suitcase
tied together with twine
in which you've stuffed
all your singular belongings.

Leave behind
a room
washed by sun
or moonlight.
There should be a chair
on which you've draped a coat
that will fit anyone.

love poem

I want to write you
a love poem as headlong
as our creek
after thaw
when we stand
on its dangerous
banks and watch it carry
with it every twig
every dry leaf and branch
in its path
every scruple
when we see it
so swollen
with runoff
that even as we watch
we must grab
each other
and step back
we must grab each
other or
get our shoes
soaked we must
grab each other

Beavers

The way beavers make
of chewed wood and grass
and boughs plastered with mud
a place to live,
so we make a place
hidden and nocturnal
no one passing by would guess was there.

Walking in the woods last week we saw
trees ringed like felled moons
where a beaver's teeth had circled,
and following the unloosed stream through underbrush
where only discarded beercans held the light,
we came across their dam
in such an unexpected place.

I went with you that day against the pull
of books and walls, and moving ahead
you tried to clear an easy path for me.
Who would think passion could survive
all the damage of wear and tear
or that habit itself could be a fire
that banked and banked never burns out?

We stood and watched a while
and just as we were giving up
saw or thought we saw
the blur of movement
under water, the flash of bristles
beneath which we knew
the softer, secret

fur must lie.
Walking home if we looked hard
we could see the first wildflowers:
bloodroot and dentaria,
as pale as the first stars
just before dark. It is believed
that beavers mate for life.

balancing act: for N.

like Chinese acrobats
we climb on

each other's
shoulders

four generations
balanced

so briefly
in time

me kneeling
on my mother's frail

shoulders
my son's ankles

hard against
my neck

his child
held in one hand high

above his head
four

of us looking out
in four

directions
hooked together

by nerve
and DNA

hurry
the lights

are going
down.

Vacation

On the quietest days,
when the sea just hovers in the background
and the light is no particular color
I forget summer,
and my ordinary life comes back to me
like a letter that has been forwarded from home.
For a moment I long for the stricter air of winter
and I finger my winter worries one by one,
finally putting them away again, like beach stones
which will lose their color slowly
deep in my pockets.
Now a single gull swooping
too low over the porch
brings me back to myself
as the light turns bottle green,
and the salt spray roses drench me in scent,
and summer closes in again.

The Ordinary Weather of Summer

In the ordinary weather of summer,
with storms rumbling from west to east
like so many freight trains hauling
their cargo of heat and rain,
the dogs sprawl on the back steps, panting,
insects assemble at every window,
and we quarrel again, bombarding
each other with small grievances,
our tempers flashing on and off
in bursts of heat lightning.
In the cooler air of morning,
we drink our coffee amicably enough
and walk down to the sea
which seems to tremble with meaning
and into which we plunge again and again.
The days continue hot.
At dusk the shadows are as blue
as the lips of the children stained
with berries or with the chill
of too much swimming.
So we move another summer closer
to our last summer together—
a time as real and implacable as the sea
out of which we come walking
on wobbly legs as if for the first time,
drying ourselves with rough towels,
shaking the water out of our blinded eyes.

A Walk Before Breakfast

Isn't this what life
could be: a walk
before breakfast with the sea
opening its chapters
of water and light,
flexing its silken muscle,
pulsing back and forth—
a kind of accompaniment
to breath? Along its rough edges
shells and small birds gather,
the rick-rack of life
in all its stages: feather
and fish bone, those sandcrabs
that we see only by their tiny
pinpricks of absence.
All summer we eat when the tug
of appetite tells us,
make love at odd moments,
the sand beneath us
as pliant as flesh.
If we refused to leave,
would our skins turn
the amber of beer glass?
Would we learn to walk always arched
into the wind, half naked
and vulnerable and tough
as seaweed, leaving behind
not footprints
but the discarded carapace
of our other life?

Erosion

We are slowly
undermined. Grain
by grain . . .
inch by inch . . .
slippage.
It happens as we watch.
The waves move their long row
of scythes over the beach.

It happens as we sleep,
the way the clock's hands
move continuously
just out of sight,
but more like an hourglass
than a clock,
for here sand
is running out.

We wake to water.
Implacably lovely
is this view
though it will swallow
us whole, soon
there will be
nothing left
but view.

We have tried a seawall.
We have tried prayer.
We have planted grasses
on the bank, small tentacles
hooks of green that catch
on nothing. For the wind
does its work, the water
does its sure work.

One day the sea will simply
take us. The children
press their faces to the glass
as if the windows were portholes,
and the house fills
with animals: two dogs,
a bird, cats—we are becoming
an ark already.

The gulls will follow
our wake.
We are made of water anyway,
I can feel it in the yielding
of your flesh, though sometimes
I think that you are sand,
moving slowly, slowly
from under me.

4. The Descent

Accidents

There is no infant
this time,
only my own life swaddled
in bandages
and handed back to me
to hold in my two arms
like any new thing,
to hold to my bruised breasts
and promise
to cherish.

The smell of cut
flowers encloses this room,
insistent as anesthetic.
It is spring.
Outside the hospital window
the first leaves have opened
their shiny blades,
and a dozen new accidents
turn over in their sleep,
waiting to happen.

Song of the Hypochondriac

The book is pain,
and as I turn
its pages

words fly out
like dark
moths:

Embolism . . .
Cardiac . . .
Metastasis.

Now the parts
of the body speak, each
in its own dialect,

having in common
only
memory.

Explore us,
beg the breasts,
trembling.

Wind me, says
the clock
in the wrist.

Try to swallow,
whispers the throat,
starting to close.

It is all a case
of bad luck,
a deadly twist

of the kaleidoscope—
a different pattern
of cells.

But the doctor simply
smiles, my intricate joints
ache,

and I go to bed
under the weight of everything
that could happen.

Degas: "Intérieur"

More has happened
in this room than we want
to know. The fires
have burned out,
and the only light left
is in details: the discarded
undergarment, the hat
draped like a dying bird
on the narrow bed, all the debris
of passion.
Against a wall the man slouches
into his own shadow
the way the rug fades
into the floorboards,
the expression on his face
equivocal. Flowers bloom
on the lampshade
but will never grow.
The woman simply waits,
her ear defined
by one jade bead.
Only the lid of the jewel box glows,
as if everything valuable
had been shut away inside.

The Angel of Death

Ingres drew her
with rudimentary breasts
and pre-pubescent wings
barely sketched in.
The hair is cropped,
the narrow eyebrows arched
into a look both thoughtful
and pitiless as only
the young can be,
who know themselves
immortal.

Snowing: A Triptych

1.

It is snowing
so lightly
the air seems blurred
with static
through which I see white
rimming the woods
like shadows on the negatives
of old pictures.
Only the cardinals flame
out of the trees
with the hard-edged
purposes
of hunger.

2.

This is pure
process,
the blinding
imperative
of physics
or art,
as a billion
anonymous
crystals—each
an artisan of light,
hurl
through the cold
air.

3.

I want to be buried
like this,
the snow falling
and falling
into the earth
until every crevice
and canyon
is filled,
as in China
when for burial
they filled the seven
openings
of the body
with white
jade.

The Accident

For a time
after the accident
everything seemed washed
in light,
and ordinary things
were like lost objects
unexpectedly retrieved
which have to be claimed again
one by one: yes,
to the bentwood chair,
to the birch by the door,
yes, to the scarred door itself,
to its knob
which had the secret glow
of an apple
in a Flemish painting.

It would have been
an almost perfect ending,
swift and unblemished,
for who could have guessed
that the road
was veneered in ice
and led to the lamppost;
or that the lamppost could be
a hidden exit,
a place where the past
and the future collide
in one barbarous flash
and only the body
is nothing,
disappearing at last
into certainty.

The weather welcomes me back
with its camellias
blasted to the roots
last winter
yet still surviving
in their shrouds
of color, flimsy but alive
for another season.

Memorial Gardens, Queens

In this tenement
of headstones, the dead
jostle each other
underground
in a perpetual
rush hour, thigh bone
to thigh bone.

Holding my breath
I drive by, dreaming
of cremation, of ashes
rising on their stems of smoke
to flower
in the empty spaces
between stars.

The Descent

My mother grows smaller
before my eyes, receding
into the past tense slowly.
It feels like an escalator down,
she whispers, half asleep.
I lean over the rail
and there are vistas,
whole histories spread out:
my own father in a landscape
where each blade of grass
cuts like an eyelash caught
in the eye, making a sharp edge
between what is known
and what is merely guessed.
Is it her childhood or mine
that glows with that light
only pain remembered
can throw? Fear is using
up the oxygen. I must
get used to the change
in the air, how thin it grows
and how strange it is that beauty
can become the ache
in the bone that proves
you are alive. Now evening
leaches the color from her face,
and in the leftover light
it is hard to see where
the descent will end,
hard to believe
it is death holding
her elbow with such care,
guiding her all the way down.

Family Tree

How many leaves
has death undone already
poplar   maple   oak

raked into funeral pyres
and burned
gathered

in empty sacks
and dragged away
larch   linden   birch

leaves like the maps
of small countries
I will never visit

palm-shaped leaves
whose life lines
have run out?

How many leaves
in the long autumn retreat
their brown uniforms crisp

has the wind
taken away
or scattered

like drying shells
at the edge
of a grassy surf

cherry   sumac   elm
tear-shaped or
burned out stars

while the trunks
of the trees grow fat
and the branches shake?

I stand on a New Year's day
unwilling to drink
to a year

that will bring me
one new life
but take another back

and I count
the leaves
walnut   ash

the chorus
of silent throats
telling again

and again
the long story
of smoke.

The Deathwatch Beetle

1.

A cardinal hurls itself
at my window all morning long,
trying so hard to penetrate
its own reflection
I almost let it in myself,
though once I saw
another red bird, crazed
by the walls of a room,
spatter its feathers
all over the house.

2.

My whole childhood is coming apart,
the last stitches
about to be ripped out
with your death,
and I will be left—ridiculous,
to write
condolence letters
to myself.

3.

The deathwatch beetle
earned its name
not from its ugliness
or our terror
of insects
but simply because of the sound
it makes, ticking.

4.

When your spirit
perfects itself,
will it escape
out of a nostril,
or through the spiral
passage of an ear?
Or is it even now battering
against your thin skull, wild
to get through, blood brother
to this crimson bird?

Elegy

Last night the moon lifted itself
on one wing
over the fields

and struggling to rise
this morning
like a hooked fish

through watery
layers
of sleep,

I know
with what difficulty
flowers

must pull themselves
all the way up
their stems.

How much easier
the free fall of snow
or leaves in their season.

All week, watching
the hospital gown
rising

and falling
with your raggedy breath,
I dreamed

not of resurrections
but of the slow, sensual
slide each night

into sleep, of dust
or newly shovelled earth
settling.

Something About the Trees

I remember what my father told me:
There is an age when you are most yourself.
He was just past fifty then,
Was it something about the trees that made him speak?

There is an age when you are most yourself.
I know more now than I did once.
Was it something about the trees that made him speak?
Only a single leaf had turned so far.

I know more now than I did once.
I used to think he'd always be the surgeon.
Only a single leaf had turned so far,
Even his body kept its secrets.

I used to think he'd always be the surgeon,
My mother was the perfect surgeon's wife.
Even his body kept its secrets.
I thought they both would live forever.

My mother was the perfect surgeon's wife,
I still can see her face at thirty.
I thought they both would live forever,
I thought I'd alway be their child.

I still can see her face at thirty.
When will I be most myself?
I thought I'd always be their child.
In my sleep it's never winter.

When will I be most myself?
I remember what my father told me.
In my sleep it's never winter.
He was just past fifty then.

5. The Imperfect Paradise

Eve, Long Afterwards

How the flesh
forgets
itself,

moving in that lush Eden
it recreates in sleep
or love

leaf by leaf, petal
by smoothed petal
so that old age becomes the dream

and the only necessity
is to live by touch
which has hardly changed,

to recognize
the scents of flowers,
which are still the same.

This is the way
out
of the world,

though at the edge
of the battlefield,
on the tongue's very tip

summer reasserts itself—
the barbed taste
of a drop of sweat, the green

of vines
around a locked
gate.

In the dark, counting
Adam's ribs,
she smiles. On a far tree

faint as a moon
cradled in branches
an apple hangs.

Fruit of the Tree

There were so many
kinds of fruit in that garden:
grapes and nectarines, plums
swelling out of their very skins,
kiwis whose ridiculous
name they had chosen, laughing.

But the apple was the color
of a hunter's moon
in whose light
it glowed as if lit up
from within.
The apple

was a mystery begging
to be solved.
Never mind the serpent.
Adam was off raking.
Eve would be the mother
of Newton and Bohr.

Years later
stockpiled in barns,
an apple could explode inward,
releasing the smell
of the whole
dying year.

Mother Eve

Of course she never was a child herself,
waking as she did one morning
full grown and perfect,
with only Adam, another innocent,
to love her and instruct.
There was no learning, step by step,
to walk, no bruised elbows or knees—
no small transgressions.
There was only the round, white mound
of the moon rising,
which could neither be suckled
nor leaned against.
And perhaps the serpent spoke
in a woman's voice, mothering.
Oh, who can blame her?

When she held her own child
in her arms, what did she make
of that new animal? Did she love Cain
too little or too much, looking down
at her now flawed body as if her rib,
like Adam's, might be gone?
In the litany of naming that continued
for children instead of plants,
no daughter is mentioned.
But generations later there was Rachel,
all mother herself, who knew
that bringing forth a child in pain
is only the start. It is losing them
(and Benjamin so young)
that is the punishment.

On the Question
of Free Will

Sometimes,
noticing the skeleton
embossed
on every leaf

and how
the lion's mouth
and antelope's neck
fit perfectly,

I wonder
at God's plan
had Eve refused
the apple.

The Animals

When I see a suckling pig turn
on the spit, its mouth around
an apple, or feel the soft
muzzle of a horse
eating a windfall from my hand,
I think about the animals
when Eden closed down,
who stole no fruit themselves.

After feeding so long
from Adam's outstretched hand
and sleeping under the mild stars,
flank to flank,
what did they do on freezing nights?
Still ignorant of nests and lairs
did they try to warm themselves
at the fiery leaves of the first autumn?

And how did they learn to sharpen
fangs and claws? Who taught them
the first lesson: that flesh
had been transformed to meat?
Tiger and Bear. Elk and Dove.
God saved them places on the Ark,
and Christ would honor them with
parables, calling himself the Lamb of God.

We train our dogs in strict obedience
at which we failed ourselves.
But sometimes the sound of barking
fills the night like distant artillery,
a sound as chilling as the bellow
of steers led up the ramps
of cattle cars whose gates swing
shut on them, as Eden's did.

The Imperfect Paradise

Seasonal

Which season is the loveliest of all?
Without a pause you smile and answer spring,
Thinking of Eden long before the fall.
I see green shrouds enclosing everything
And choose instead the chaos of the snow
Before God separated dark from light.
I hear the particles of matter blow
Through wintry landscapes on a wintry night.
You find the world a warm and charming place,
My Adam, you name everything in sight.
I find a garden of conspicuous waste—
The apple's flesh is cold and hard and white.
Still, at your touch my house warms to the eaves
As autumn torches all the fragile leaves.

In the Garden

How do we tell the flowers from the weeds
Now that the old equality of space
Has ended in the garden, and the seeds
Of milkweed and daisy scatter in disgrace?
Is it the stamen, petal, or the leaf
That like the ancient signature of Cain
Marks the flesh of wildflowers, to their grief
Just as the orchid blossoms into fame?
And Esau was the wildflower of his clan,
And Jacob was the brother who was chosen.
So we learn to distinguish man from man
Like botanists, our categories frozen.
But in a single morning roses die
While dandelions and chokeweed multiply.

Deep in these Woods

Darling, how do you make your garden grow
Deep in these woods, drowning in so much shade
That even hardy May apples are slow
To rise above the shadows where they wade?
Are you a threat to every living tree?
We lean against two trunks, resting our backs
But though your craggy face is what I see
I know that somewhere you conceal an axe.
When he planned Eden did great God conceive
Flowers that flourish with no need of light?
And was there nothing Adam hid from Eve?
And doesn't the cereus bloom at night?
You place a burst of lilac in my hand
And sacrifice an oak. I almost understand.

Thief

You caught a thieving squirrel in your trap
And for the sake of cardinal and jay
You put it, fat with birdseed, in a sack
And carried it a full five miles away.
Today there is another squirrel there
Or else, more likely, this one is the same,
Making its way through all the clues of air
Along the highway 'til it found our name.
Is this a metaphor for what we feel,
Pushing our nibbling doubts five miles from sight?
Boredom and passion, alternately real,
Pull us apart, then stagger us with light.
The animals of marriage are as wild,
hungry, and stubborn as any squirrel's child.

The Imperfect Paradise

If God had stopped work after the fifth day
With Eden full of vegetables and fruits,
If oak and lilac held exclusive sway
Over a kingdom made of stems and roots,
If landscape were the genius of creation
And neither man nor serpent played a role
And God must look to wind for lamentation
And not to picture postcards of the soul,
Would he have rested on his bank of cloud
With nothing in the universe to lose,
Or would he hunger for a human crowd?
Which would a wise and just creator choose:
The green hosannas of a budding leaf
Or the strict contract between love and grief?

Somewhere in the Euphrates

Somewhere in the Euphrates, buried, lost
The rusted gates of Eden still remain,
And archeologists at awful cost
Search for a snakeskin or an apple stain,
Talk of Atlantis and the walls of Troy
As if they had to prove each legend real
Or else, like fools of science, must destroy
Geographies of what we only feel.
While sometimes watching at the window here
I see you in the garden on your knees;
It is as close as you have come to prayer,
Planting the shadblow and the peonies,
Making azaleas, hollies, dogwoods grow,
Digging up Eden with a single hoe.